Walking on Water

Jonathan Imbody

ISBN: 9798744303853

DEDICATION

Dedicated to Amy--my wife and spiritual co-adventurer.

Walking on Water

Scriptural principles for transformative living.

Table of Contents

Introduction

Followers of Christ who know the Scriptures hear of the abundant life and see God's power in His transformed disciples…Peter, Mary Magdalene, Paul, the Gerasene demoniac, Matthew the tax collector and many more.

But do we ourselves *experience* the abundant life and see God's amazing power in our daily lives? Do we "walk by the Spirit" in a life of faith-filled adventures? Or do we instead limit our risks to carefully calculated ventures easily accomplished through our own natural abilities?

A clear apprehension of the difference between natural and supernatural abilities can put us on a path to transformation. We begin that transformation when we understand and accept that in God's kingdom, striving in our mere natural abilities accomplishes *nothing*. Only as we humbly yield ourselves to Christ in faith, and He fills us with His life and the power of His Holy Spirit, can we accomplish anything.

And in Christ we can *accomplish anything.*

In our natural abilities, we can't even seem to stop worrying, love our enemies or overcome our fears, much less raise the dead, cast out demons and rejoice in the midst of persecution as the first disciples did. Jesus' disciples were frail and flawed human beings just like you and I. Yet they lived transformed lives of amazing power.

They had witnessed and learned the truth that following and imitating Christ *all depends upon God*: His power, His grace, His Spirit.

We see in a single moment this stark contrast of natural versus supernatural living--when Peter leaves a storm-wracked boat and walks on water to come to Jesus. For a glorious moment, Peter puts his faith in Christ alone and experiences the nature-transcending power of God.

Peter walks on water.

But then panic prompts him to take his eyes off Jesus. Forgetting faith and focusing instead on his limited natural abilities, he begins to sink.

Still, that brief, glorious moment shows us that we can, through faith in Christ, walk on water.

In fact, *all of the Christian life is walking on water.*

The following study of Scripture mixed with brief narratives will guide you through fundamental yet neglected principles of living the Christian life—the life that God transformed us to live. If you have "ears to hear," you will hear Him calling you through His Word to a deeper, more abundant, powerful and spiritually fruitful life.

May God quicken His Word to you and equip you to live the walk-on-water life.

We can focus on our natural limitations or on God's supernatural power.

Peter illustrates the natural or the spiritual lives we can choose to live.

The faith and failures, betrayals and courage of Peter show us the difference between depending on our natural perspective and depending in faith on the Spirit of the living God.

And He said, "Come!"
And Peter got out of the boat, and walked on the water and came toward Jesus.
--Matthew 14:29

Peter literally stepped out in faith, and he literally walked on water. He chose to live, if only for a glorious moment, the extraordinary, supernatural life that God bids us to experience if we only believe.

But seeing the wind, he became frightened, and beginning to sink, he cried out, "Lord, save me!" Immediately Jesus stretched out His hand and took hold of him, and said to him, "You of little faith, why did you doubt?"
--Matthew 14:30-31

When Peter took his eyes off Jesus and focused instead on his natural limitations and the strong forces arrayed against him, he slipped off his faith path and sank.

When Jesus exhorts Peter to believe, He is driving him toward a victorious life of greater faith and success.

Focus on the faith—not the floundering.

Anyone inclined to criticize Peter for failing in faith and flailing in the water might first ask himself, "When is the last time *I* walked on water?"

Is it not exceedingly better to step out in faith and walk on water, even if we might flounder, than to cling to the boat and never experience God's supernatural power?

God can transform us as Jesus lives within us.

Jesus answered and said to him, "Truly, truly, I say to you, unless one is born again he cannot see the kingdom of God."
--John 3:3

When we confess and turn from our sins--admitting the utter inadequacy of the self-life, submitting to God and placing our faith in Christ--we enter into a new relationship with God. No longer separated by our sin from a holy God, we are joined together as a family. We are *born again*. God makes us a brand new creature.

Therefore if anyone is in Christ, he is a new creature; the old things passed away; behold, new things have come.
--2 Corinthians 5:17

God does not merely reform us with a new code of living; He *transforms* us with His own *divine life*.

Moreover, I will give you a new heart and put a new spirit within you; and I will remove the heart of stone from your flesh and give you a heart of flesh. I will put My Spirit within you and cause you to walk in My statutes, and you will be careful to observe My ordinances.
--Ezekiel 36:26-27

The very person of Jesus Christ comes to indwell us by the power of the Holy Spirit.

If Christ is in you, though the body is dead because of sin, yet the spirit is alive because of righteousness.
--Romans 8:10

I have been crucified with Christ; and it is no longer I who live, but Christ lives in me; and the life which I now live in the flesh I live by faith in the Son of God, who loved me and gave Himself up for me.
--Galatians 2:20

The life that indwells us—Jesus Christ Himself, by His Holy Spirit—enables us to escape the bounds of the natural realm and experience the limitless power of the divine.

But if the Spirit of Him who raised Jesus from the dead dwells in you, He who raised Christ Jesus from the dead will also give life to your mortal bodies through His Spirit who dwells in you.
--Romans 8:11

God calls us to live in a supernatural Kingdom.

As we begin our new life in Christ, He opens our eyes to the supernatural Kingdom in which we live. Like Christ, who is our life, we no longer remain bound to the natural, limited physical realm. Situationally, we have left the kingdom of this world and have entered the glorious, eternal Kingdom of God.

"For God so loved the world, that He gave His only begotten Son,
that whoever believes in Him shall not perish, but have eternal life.
--John 3:16

As a result, our new life in this new dimension should be vastly *different* than the lethally limited existence we experienced while trapped in our sins and mortal bodies in the kingdom of this world. Yes, we still live in those bodies and we still walk on this earth, but we have taken on an invisible new spiritual dimension.

Spiritually speaking, we now live where Christ lives—in the heavenly Kingdom.

Therefore if you have been raised up with Christ, keep seeking the things above,
where Christ is, seated at the right hand of God.
--Colossians 3:1

Whether or not we actually *experience* that limitless life, whether or not we actually *claim* our incredible inheritance, depends on the realization and actualization, by faith, of our new position in Christ.

We choose daily whether to attempt to live as the old, dead natural man or to truly live as a new, living spiritual creation.

Set your mind on the things above, not on the things that are on earth. For you have died and your life is hidden with Christ in God.
--Colossians 3:2-3

We can choose either fleshly futility or supernatural success.

We can relate to Peter's believing and then faltering. We, like Peter, choose on some days to walk by faith in God and on other days to futilely depend on ourselves.

Simon Peter answered, "You are the Christ, the Son of the living God."
And Jesus said to him, "Blessed are you, Simon Barjona, because flesh and blood did not reveal this to you, but My Father who is in heaven.
I also say to you that you are Peter, and upon this rock I will build My church;
and the gates of Hades will not overpower it."
--Matthew 16:16-19

When Peter confessed Jesus as the Son of God, he sensed and followed the leading of the Holy Spirit, received His truth and aligned his belief with God. He stepped into the spiritual realm by opening the door of faith.

But we need to keep the door of faith open, or sin and doubt will slam shut our spiritual experience.

Then he began to curse and swear, "I do not know the man!" And immediately a rooster crowed. And Peter remembered the word which Jesus had said, "Before a rooster crows, you will deny Me three times." And he went out and wept bitterly.
--Matthew 26:74 - 27:1

After his wonderful, spiritually discerned pronouncement ("You are the Christ"), Peter sinks once again into fleshly failure ("I do not know the man"). We likewise can walk backward out of the spiritual realm and into the natural realm.

This happens as we yield to "the sin which so easily entangles us" (Hebrews 12:1) and indulge our weak, natural impulses of fear, lust, greed, hatred and other temptations.

Make no mistake: though common, such lapses from the spiritual into the natural are by no means inevitable. In our new spiritual nature, God has empowered us to *overcome* all temptation.

No temptation has overtaken you but such as is common to man; and God is faithful, who will not allow you to be tempted beyond what you are able, but with the temptation will provide the way of escape also, so that you will be able to endure it.
--1 Corinthians 10:13

We can do nothing of worth apart from Christ

Jesus clearly contrasts the absolute difference between living in relationship with and depending upon God versus living merely in the natural realm. The choice, He makes clear to us, is not a matter of degree, as if the natural path is fine while the supernatural path is simply incrementally better.

No, Jesus says; our choice is a *binary* one:

Abide in Me, and I in you. As the branch cannot bear fruit of itself unless it abides in the vine, so neither can you unless you abide in Me. I am the vine, you are the branches; he who abides in Me and I in him, he bears much fruit, for apart from Me you can do nothing.
--John 15:4-5

An ordinary person can lead an extraordinary life.

Upon the rock of faith—the same faith that Peter expressed in his confession of Jesus as God—Christ builds His Church through those who put their trust in Him.

> "*...you also, as living stones, are being built up as a spiritual house for a holy priesthood, to offer up spiritual sacrifices acceptable to God through Jesus Christ.*
> --1 Peter 2:5

By such faith, an otherwise ordinary person in whom Christ lives can lead an *extraordinary* life. A naturally fearful person can overcome fear to accomplish great achievements. A person who has tragically failed according to the measure of the world can find unbridled success in the Kingdom of God. A person of uncontrolled temper and constant conflict can experience and share "the peace of God, which surpasses all comprehension" (Philippians 4:7).

This amazing, supernatural path of victory is the *normal* Christian life. Our life is *all* walking on water.

Some days—perhaps especially when we recognize our weakness and personal inadequacy—we realize this truth and rely on God to sustain, strengthen and equip us. We rest in His peace, knowing He has the power to deliver us from the waves that seem poised to overwhelm us.

Other days—often after the rough winds and waves subside—we drift back into relying on our natural selves, neglecting our reliance on God for our very breath. We settle for so much less than the abundant, triumphant life our Father wants for us and for which His Son died to make available to us.

This life is extraordinary and supernatural, explainable only by an infusion of the power of the living God.

Now to Him who is able to do far more abundantly beyond all that we ask or think, according to the power that works within us, to Him be the glory in the church and in Christ Jesus to all generations forever and ever.
--Ephesians 3:20-21

The kingdom of God is more than character and values.

God clearly commands us to adopt His values and align our thinking with His principles, to change our behavior in the direction of His righteousness. This obedience and moral character formation are foundational to the Christian life.

But adopting God's values and changing our behavior *are not the ultimate goal*; they are a means to an end. That end is experiencing a *relationship* with God and living the abundant life in Jesus Christ.

"*I came that they may have life, and have it abundantly.*"
John 10:10

The Christian life includes but is so more than fellowship, more than right living, more than sound doctrine, more than avoiding temptation.

The Christian life is *experiencing the love of God, the peace of Christ and the fellowship of the Holy Spirit.*

Experiencing this supernatural life, we can soar above the constraints of human nature, tap into the power of the living God and accomplish what we could not naturally accomplish. Through the testimony of our lives that offer an aroma of Christ, we also can lead others to the Kingdom of God.

We can experience an abundant life.

Yet so many of us don't actually *experience* the abundant life on a daily basis. The "abundant life" may seem at times more like an advertising slogan than a potent description of our own reality.

So we content ourselves with the benefits of aligning our values, behavior and thoughts with God's principles. We enjoy companionable potlucks with fellow congregants but not deep, spiritual fellowship. We achieve a level of success in our work that is merely commensurate with our natural abilities, education and training. We love those who are loveable, we limit our risks to assured results and we attempt to persuade skeptics merely with reasoned arguments.

Of course, aligning our lives with God's principles actually does yield tangible benefits in this world. We avoid many calamities that result from ignoring God's principles. We enjoy a general peace of mind knowing that we are in a right relationship with God and headed toward a happy ending.

But this generally contented life that comes from aligning with God's principles *does not come close* to matching the promises, the invitations and evidences we see in the Scriptures.

And behold, I am sending forth the promise of My Father upon you; but you are to stay in the city until you are clothed with power from on high."
Luke 24:49

When the day of Pentecost had come, they were all together in one place. And suddenly there came from heaven a noise like a violent rushing wind, and it filled the whole house where they were sitting. And there appeared to them tongues as of fire distributing themselves, and they rested on each one of them. And they were all filled with the Holy Spirit and began to speak with other tongues, as the Spirit was giving them utterance.

--Acts 2:1-4

That spiritual power at Pentecost transformed Peter from an unfaithful fisherman into an intrepid leader of a spiritual revolution that turned the world upside down.

But Peter, taking his stand with the eleven, raised his voice and declared to them….

"Therefore let all the house of Israel know for certain that God has made Him both Lord and Christ—this Jesus whom you crucified."

--Acts 2:14, 36

After Peter spoke with amazing power and boldness, thousands repented, gave their lives to Christ and experienced the new birth. All this came about just days after a terrified, faithless Peter had sworn, "I do not know the man!"

The difference between Pentecost and today is *power*.

All the clever sermons, all the restructuring of our church services to make them "seeker friendly," all the seminaries churning out socially sensitive clergy, all the marketing techniques, all the smoke-pumping, bass-reverberating worship services do not come close to the power of Pentecost.

None of these techniques and devices can ever compensate for a *lack of spiritual power.*

Only the power of the Holy Spirit, as He lives and speaks through humble and faith-filled servants, can yield a spiritual harvest such as witnessed in the days of the early Church.

And when I came to you, brethren, I did not come with superiority of speech or of wisdom, proclaiming to you the testimony of God. For I determined to know nothing among you except Jesus Christ, and Him crucified.
I was with you in weakness and in fear and in much trembling, and my message and my preaching were not in persuasive words of wisdom, but in demonstration of the Spirit and of power, so that your faith would not rest on the wisdom of men, but on the power of God.
--1 Corinthians 2:1-5

Such powerful preaching is walking on water. Helping others find the path to God depends wholly on God's power—not on our clever devices—to transform lives.

When we cannot even get our children to pick up their clothes, convince our spouses to see things our way or persuade our supervisors to reward us according to our estimation, what in the world makes us think we are clever or charming enough to lead a skeptic to believe the mystery of the Gospel? How can we possibly hope in our own abilities to convince someone that God came to earth as a man to die for our sins, then rose from the dead and ascended to heaven, from where He will one day return for us?

Just as the conversion of ice to water requires heat, the supernatural conversion of a person from a natural enemy of God into a spiritual member of God's family requires *divine power*. Earthly medicine can heal the body, but only heavenly power can heal both body and soul.

The kingdom of God is more than a life insurance policy.

We experience God's power when we not only believe in Him but also believe "that He is a *rewarder* of those who *seek* Him" (Hebrews 11:6).

If we think of salvation—our coming to Christ by faith—merely in dry legal, covenantal terms by which we secure a contract for a future home in heaven, we miss out on the *living relationship* God wants for us now.

Why settle for a life insurance policy for heaven when God offers you a heavenly life with Him *now*?

He wants to literally live within us, filling our deepest being. He wants to fill us with His Holy Spirit, the very Spirit of Christ, the Spirit of God's power.

Faith is not the goal but a means to an end.

We can experience this life through faith--the key to the kingdom of heaven, the rock on which Jesus builds His church. Faith helps us establish a relationship with God, as we repent of ourselves and embrace God Himself as our King.

Yet even faith is not the goal. Like right living and moral character, faith is a means to an end. One who places faith in Christ does not merely become a person of faith as opposed to a person without hope. The believer now can experience *life* with God through Christ, in the *power* of His Holy Spirit.

Faith triggers God's deep and miraculous *transformation* of us from within. How we live our daily lives changes as we walk in the Spirit. We exchange our own feeble ability for His Spirit's ability, for His power to move mountains, to raise the dead to life, to transform the earthly into the heavenly and the mortal into the immortal.

In daily, concrete ways, that means we trust God to work things out that we can't work out with our own smarts. We forgive our enemies when our feelings demand revenge. We persevere in serving a loved one when we're sick and tired of helping. We keep walking with God even when life seems the opposite of what we wanted and we have no idea what He is doing.

We can all walk on water.

If it seems that a walk-on-water life requires a ton of faith, we can take heart that Jesus encourages us to start small:

Then the disciples came to Jesus privately and said, "Why could we not drive it out?"
And He said to them, "Because of the littleness of your faith; for truly I say to you, if you have faith the size of a mustard seed, you will say to this mountain, 'Move from here to there,' and it will move; and nothing will be impossible to you."
--Matthew 17:20

Living a walk-on-water life doesn't require a mountain of faith; it requires an all-powerful God. Start small, start believing that God can do what you cannot. Step out of the boat in faith. Ask God to provide you with opportunities and the faith and courage to walk on water.

How can a follower of Jesus start walking on water?

1. Confess to God that you have limited your lackluster Christian life by relying on the natural rather than the supernatural.

2. Express your desire for more—the walk-on-water life that comes by living in God's power and His supernatural kingdom.

3. Ask God to *help* you believe and not doubt, to exchange fear for courage, depression for confidence, hatred for love.

4. Submit unreservedly to God and ask Him to *fill* you afresh with His Holy Spirit, with new *power*, with His very *life*.

If you have not yet given your life to Christ and want to experience the spiritual rebirth and abundant new life that He offers:

1. Recognize that your sin has separated you from God, *"for all have sinned and fall short of the glory of God"* (Romans 3:23).

2. Realize that because God loves you, Jesus paid the price for your sins on the cross: *"But God demonstrates His own love toward us, in that while we were yet sinners, Christ died for us"* (Romans 5:8).

3. Know that although *"the wages of sin is death," "the free gift of God is eternal life in Christ Jesus our Lord"* (Romans 6:23).

4. Act on God's promise *"that if you confess with your mouth Jesus as Lord, and believe in your heart that God raised Him from the dead, you will be saved"* (Romans 10:9).

As you confess your sin and receive God's forgiveness and new life through His Son Jesus Christ, He will begin to transform you. You can accelerate that transformation by:

- beginning to learn more about your new life by reading in the Bible the books of John and Romans;

- finding a fellowship of believers who gather together in a church that honors God's Word, to help strengthen your faith and provide you with opportunities to love and serve others;

- receiving water baptism as a public sign that you have become a new creation in Christ;

- asking God to fill you with His Spirit, who now lives in you, for the power to live the supernatural, "walk on water" life.

God invites us to share in the life, death and resurrection of Christ. May we follow the path of our Lord Jesus and experience the abundant life He has prepared for us. May it be true of us just as it was true of our Lord when the angels said,

"Why do you seek the living One among the dead? He is not here, but He has risen."
--Luke 24:5-6

My Notes

My Notes

ABOUT THE AUTHOR

A veteran writer of over four decades, Jonathan Imbody has authored *Faith Steps*, which encourages and equips Christians to engage in public policy issues. He also has published over 100 commentaries in *The Washington Post, USA Today, New York Times, Los Angeles Times, San Francisco Chronicle, Chicago Sun-Times* and many other national publications. *World* magazine featured his essay summarizing the major medical accomplishments and challenges of the past millennium.

As an expert in federal government relations, Jonathan has participated in over 40 White House meetings and events. He has testified on euthanasia and assisted suicide before a U.S. Senate committee.

Jonathan received his bachelor's degree in journalism and speech communications from the Pennsylvania State University, a master's degree from Penn State in counseling and education and a certificate in biblical and theological studies from the Alliance Theological Seminary in New York. His wife Amy founded the Center for Redemptive Education. Jonathan and Amy have four children and five grandchildren.

Made in the USA
Middletown, DE
17 November 2021